Without You,
I Would Be Nothing

ALSO BY BROOKE L. DAVIS

Adventures of an Urban Homesteader

WITHOUT YOU,
I WOULD BE NOTHING

100 Micro-Memoirs

Brooke L. Davis

Gallatin River Press

Published by Gallatin River Press, Highlands Ranch, CO.

This book is memoir. It reflects the author's present recollections of experiences over time. Some names and characteristics have been changed, some events have been compressed, and some dialogue has been recreated.

Copyright © 2021 Brooke L Davis

Cover photograph courtesy of the author
Cover design by Brandi McCann
Print and eBook book design by Victoria Wolf

Library of Congress Control Number: 2021912879

ISBN Paperback 978-1-7366758-0-9
ISBN eBook 978-1-7366758-1-6

To those who came before,
know you are not forgotten.

Contents

Everybody Wants to Rule the World 1980-1985

True Colors 1986-1992

Welcome to the Jungle 1993-2014

Slip Slidin' Away 2015-Present

Without You,
I Would Be Nothing

A Note to Readers

This project is what happens when the concepts behind Grant Faulkner's *Fissures* and Beth Ann Fennelly's *Heating & Cooling* make a baby. It's the result of me walking through my living room one day and thinking, *Huh, I should write a micro-memoir like Beth Ann, but also challenge myself to make each memoir one hundred words like Grant did in his book of stories. I'm sure that's been done before, but it sounds fun (and masochistic).*

My I-should-make-a-book-baby thought led to an excess of negative self-talk that nearly squashed the birth of said baby. I started this project several years ago, and about midway through, almost gave up. Who would want to read about my life? What did I have to share that would resonate with others? I grew up in the Midwest, and Indiana isn't exactly New York or Los Angeles. I discovered that place was a large part of my story, as was growing up in the seventies and eighties when the hair was big, the colors were bright, and the music was epic.

As I wrote and the final form of this book took shape, I came to believe that *everyone* should recount their lives this way. It's challenging to compose meaningful memoirs in one hundred words. It's also challenging to come up with one hundred memories you want to share. My brain felt like it was being mashed through a strainer as I struggled to dial up the last twenty-five vignettes I needed to reach a full one hundred.

One thing writing this micro-memoir brought into glaring focus was that we never know what's around the corner or how much time we have left. I don't live in fear of either of those things, but being alive for a half century has taught me to respect the Big Clock as it ticks on. The Grim Reaper is coming (not to be morbid—and this micro-memoir isn't—but #truthbomb: dude in the black hood holding a scythe will tap us all on the shoulder with a bony finger one of these years) and eventually, he always gets his way.

My intent with this micro-memoir was to highlight the things that made me who I am: experiences, family, and place. Experiences shape us far more than we realize, for good or ill. Families are people bound to us by blood and other (sometimes dubious) associations. Places touch us, hold us, and form us whether we live there or not.

Because of the personal nature of this collection, I wrote it as if you and I were sitting at a table enjoying a beverage (you choose the type, depending on your mood), recounting the funny, heartwarming, and sometimes tragic things that happen over a lifetime. While reading, you may want to have tissues on hand. Most of all, I hope these vignettes inspire you to reflect on the experiences that shaped you and who you would be without them.

Disclaimer: This book is memoir. It reflects my memories of experiences over time. Some names have been changed and some events have been compressed. Please remember that references and situations from the seventies and eighties may be interpreted differently today than they were then; I tried to stay true to my youthful recollections as I told my story.

You Are the Sunshine of My Life
1971–1979

Knock on Wood

On April 7, 1971, I kicked myself off the couch to help my mom take out the trash. At three months old, I couldn't walk but was curious and wanted to follow her to the garage. There was a thump (thank God for the Oriental rug covering the hardwood floor) and loud wailing. My horrified mother rushed back inside, comforted me, and wouldn't let me sleep because she thought I might have a head injury. I didn't. Now when I leap off the couch, I risk cracking my knees on the coffee table instead of my head on the floor.

Warp Speed

My father handed me up to the lady wrangler at the tender age of two, and away we trotted down the gravel road outside the corral at the Montana ranch where my family was staying. I surveyed the world from what felt like a hundred feet up, yet remained safe as we bumped and lurched past hayfields that melted into the distant foothills. That first ride was the start of my love affair with horses and the west. Sure-footed animals with velvety noses carried me into beautiful wildernesses. In later years, I hid my tears when I had to leave.

Balded by Love

As a toddler, I loved Suzie Doll so much that the hair on the back of her head wore off and she was left with a scratchy, cropped, bristle-brush–like mohawk. I carried her around in a headlock and napped with her every day in my crib. My mother sewed colorful cotton print dresses for her and patched her worn body twice in ecru muslin. Suzie traveled in high (suitcase) style to Michigan, Montana, and California. As with love and comfort, there are possessions we can't live without, and Suzie's hair was the price she paid for being my everything.

Big Red and Little Black

One of my favorite books when I was a small child was *Little Black, A Pony*. It's the tale of a once-favored pony who runs away because he can't run, jump, swim, or keep up with Big Red, his young master's new horse. But when the boy and Big Red fall through the ice on a frozen lake, it's Little Black who saves them. In times of discouragement or disappointment, I sometimes think of Little Black and remember that I have value even though I'm different. Like Little Black, each one of us is made to do things others can't.

Without a Scratch

At four, I rushed toward a storm door on my way to the swing set, and when I reached for the latch, I missed. My hand shattered the glass and went clean through. Instinctively, I yanked my hand back, avoided the jagged shards, and walked away uninjured. Management at the Michigan motel lodge where my father was fly-fishing was positive I'd done it on purpose. I never cried, and my relieved parents paid for a new door. I still rush toward blue skies and swing sets, but now I'm more conscious of imaginary boundaries that try to contain my spirit.

Asleep on the Landing

One evening when I was little I didn't quite make it to bed. I climbed all the way up our baby-blue carpeted stairs, but when I reached the landing I was too tired to conquer the last two steps and the short walk to my bedroom. Even the promise of plush stuffed animals and snuggly blankets couldn't keep me from lying down next to a giant potted plant to rest my eyes. My mother found me later, fast asleep, and tucked me in. She still thinks this qualifies as a Bad Mom moment, but I've tried to convince her otherwise.

Glamour Girl

My parents were part of the bridge-playing seventies set. Before they'd go out for the evening, I'd watch my mother apply her makeup and beg her to let me try one of her Merle Norman lipstick samplers. Each sampler was an inch long and the diameter of a pencil, a perfect size for my fingers. Because I was only tall enough to see my eyes in the mirror, I'd dab on the creamy lipstick, stand on my tiptoes, and crane my head up to see my lips. Sometimes I'd smear the lipstick on straight and look pretty, just like Mom.

Locked In

When I was five, I accidentally locked myself in our upstairs linen closet. I sat cross-legged below the lowest shelf and made sure I could reach the doorknob when the door was almost closed—but with the door completely closed and latched, my arm wouldn't fit between it and the shelf. I cried and cried until my mom found me. After she let me out, I never played in that dreaded closet again. Sometimes the best hiding places turn out to be prisons, not sanctuaries. When Mom can't come to the rescue, you have to escape the darkness by yourself.

Early Lesson

One day during the steamy summer before I attended kindergarten, Dad stopped the John Deere and let it idle near the lake, but I knew he wasn't finished mowing. When he came to get me, I thought I might get to ride on the tractor. Instead, we crept through the cattails at the water's edge until a tiny fawn, white spots gleaming, appeared, laying stock-still on a pile of flattened reeds. My father told me never to touch a baby deer, because its mother would smell me and abandon it. Simple advice often means the difference between life and death.

Bicentennial 1976

America celebrated its bicentennial in 1976 with a live televised parade in Philadelphia. My mother told me to watch part of it because it was a special day for our country, and something I'd never see again. Being dutiful, I agreed (despite wanting to watch Captain Kangaroo). The marching bands strutted and blasted, baton twirlers twisted, sequin-clad dancers gyrated, and patriotic floats adorned with colorful carnations rolled down the street. When you're young, you don't understand what it means to be told you'll never see something again. Now I'm not young and I understand. I'm glad she made me watch.

Indoor Gardening

We were busted because we were giggling. But giggling is what precocious six-year-olds do when they're elbow-deep in dirt, transplanting a tall houseplant from the stair landing into a bathroom sink. Lisa the neighbor girl and I were hauling handfuls of soil up two steps, through my bedroom, and (according to my mother) flinging them into my sink. To say we got in trouble doesn't begin to cover it, and yes, the gigglers had to clean up the mess. After that, I was told I could only play in the dirt *outside*...where I soon accidentally unearthed my father's tulip bulbs.

A Violet for Your Chicken Pox

My father gifted me an African violet when I had chicken pox in the first grade. I was a feverish itchy seven-year-old trying not to squirm on a couch, and he wanted to brighten my day. Dad and I liked plants, so buying me a violet when I had flowering skin was a win-win. Those dainty blossoms and silken leaves graced that violet for almost twenty years. Looking back, this should've been my first clue that my father's care wasn't always expressed through words, but through a shared love of nature, the appreciation of beautiful colors, and lasting unspoken gestures.

Through the Wringer

Pan one held the soapy water and agitator. Pan two was for rinsing. Clothes were washed in the same water—cleanest first, farm clothes last because they were the dirtiest—then run through the wringer into the rinse water, where they were sloshed as needed. Rinsed clothes ran through the wringer into a basket to be hung outside to dry. Laundry with my grandmother was a practical adventure in planning, sorting, and hanging items on the clothesline. Joy was often found in mundane tasks when I was young, even if the dry sheets were scratchy and stiff as a board.

Bright Shiny Objects

As a child, I was fascinated with the silvery insides of freshly gutted fish. I'd watch from a safe distance as my father fileted the largemouth bass with a razor-sharp knife, then I'd come close and he'd hand me the glimmering strips of innards that shone like tinsel. I was the weird little girl who cared more about shiny fish guts than eating the fish. Sadly, the strips shriveled up when I tried to preserve them by burying them in my sandbox. I'm still distracted by shiny things, and sometimes mourn when their sparkle and allure fades and they die.

All the Pretty Yellow Roses

I first met death briefly when I was eight and my papaw died. Because the two sides of my family have vastly different opinions about how old young people should be before they're allowed to view the deceased, I wasn't present for the open-casket portion of his funeral. When I walked past my papaw's closed casket covered with an enormous spray of yellow roses, I thought it was the most beautiful box I'd ever seen. I don't have a final lasting memory of him, but seeing him in an open casket surrounded by those roses would've been a good one.

Seventies Child

Kids today are hermetically sealed in bubble wrap before they're allowed to have fun, but no one parented this way in the seventies, and most of us are still alive. My cousins and I played in haymows so high we would've broken our necks had we fallen on the perilous climb down. My friends and I never had bike helmets; we had ponytail bands and the wind in our hair. I rode a 50cc motorbike helmetless and rarely fell off. It wasn't that our parents didn't care; it was just a different time...and we always knew not to get hurt.

We Didn't Have Those in Southern Indiana

The wife of a man in my father's national fisherpeople organization epitomized seventies glamour to a young and impressionable me. She looked like Pam from *Urban Cowboy*, with long onyx hair, but instead of being a haughty cowgirl she was boho chic, with flowy vibrant maxi-dresses and a casual air of smooth sophistication. She and her husband worked a room with laughter and ease and never let their endless glasses of scotch render them tipsy. I wanted to recreate her breezy and confident style, but I knew I never could because we didn't have women like her where I lived.

Traveling in Style

I miss the carefree years when I was short enough to sleep lying down in the back seat of our 1975 evergreen Monte Carlo with tan interior. Like all good mothers of that era, my mom kept our car ready for when I needed to do some cozy nighttime snoozing. I had a pillow and a homemade reversible yellow check and print blanket that was as long as the seat. Sometimes I'd change into my Winnie the Pooh footie pj's in the car before I lay down to sleep. The miles fly by fast when you're dreaming in toasty warmth.

Everybody Wants to
Rule the World
1980-1985

Sugar High

When Mom and I made my birthday cake in 1980, we learned how fast you could lose your grip on a mixing bowl with the hand mixer set on high. Not only did we frost the cake, but we also frosted the kitchen, including the carpet—which is bad when you live in a rental. I wiped a tragic waste of chocolate off the cupboards while my mother stood on the counter and dabbed at the ceiling. To this day, we keep a firm hand on the mixing bowl, check the backsplash for splatters, and still laugh about flying frosting.

That Pioneer Spirit

The winter we lived in our rental with its enormous metal statue of a Roman chariot race, we had to park my father's 1978 Ford Ranchero outside. One frigid morning, Dad returned inside and announced he was taking Mom's Buick because the truck window had disintegrated when he closed the door. Glass indeed turns to pixie dust below certain temperatures. Mom and I bundled up under blankets and blasted the heater on our daily drives to and from school until the window was repaired. I loved pretending I was Laura Ingalls Wilder rolling across the prairie in a burgundy wagon.

What Lies Beneath

When we moved to the country—its rolling grassy hills edged in maples—my grandfather worried I'd drown in our sixteen-acre lake. Luckily, his fear never materialized; I held no fascination for the water and had already learned to swim in town, safe in a backyard pool. Trumpeter swans and Canadian geese often nested in the secluded end of the lake near the hardwood forest. I watched the adults shepherd their young each season, always heartbroken when one went missing. Life is precarious, not just for wildlife, and I think my grandfather knew I could be lost in an instant.

Adventures with Fisherpeople

Because my father was an officer in a large national fish conservation organization in the early eighties, we visited exotic places like upstate New York, where retired people played bocce and I played with other fisher-family kids. Jennifer, who had one leg shorter than the other, wore a thick-soled black shoe so she could walk normally and never let her affliction slow her down. Her ordinary parents suddenly became glamourous when I discovered they traveled with their own liquor cabinet. I always wondered if their drinking had anything to do with her leg, but I'm sure it was just genetics.

Arithmetic on My Fingers

Because I could never memorize basic addition and subtraction, I had to solve math test problems with my fingers. This was unceremoniously brought to my (and my parents') attention by my third-grade teacher.

She said, "Brooke smacks her pencil down on the desk, counts on her fingers, and then picks the pencil back up to answer the problem."

Telling on me was a big mistake. After that, I kept ahold of my pencil and counted on my other hand under the desk. My teacher never noticed, and I still count on my fingers and do other things you can't see.

Kick 'Em in the Shins

To show her support, my aunt sent my cousin Michael to kindergarten in cowboy boots and told him that if he was bullied, to kick that little boy in the shins. She soon ended up in the principal's office, where she assured him she'd authorized the kicking because the school hadn't come up with a better solution. That bully never bothered Michael again. As a third grader, this episode immediately qualified my aunt as one badass mother, and I envied Mike because my mom would never have done that. Sometimes, boots and Mom are all you need to feel invincible.

Hiding in Plain Sight

When you're ten and your family has more than the other families in your rural community, all you want is to fit in and not let anyone see where you live. You wear jeans and gray sweatshirts and have the same insecurities as everyone else. You refine the social art form of quick comebacks on the school bus and assure others you don't have servants or live in a castle. Witnessing poverty humbles you. Farm-raised parents help. I knew character, trust, and friendships couldn't be purchased, but years later I regretted the time I'd wasted trying to conform and hide.

When California Was Tahiti

My mom and I visited my aunt and uncle in California the year their youngest son was born. They lived in a Craftsman-style house on a half-acre lot in North Hollywood and had an in-ground pool, a hot tub, and two giant tortoises who hibernated in large holes. We picked tart lemons and juicy grapefruit with a long-handled picker from trees in their backyard. With temps in the sixties, we might as well have been in Tahiti. Indiana winters are five months of dreary twenty-degree weather. When we got back home, what I missed most was that ever-present golden sun.

Walk the Line

Everyone who lived on our road knew that the families that filtered through the single-story rental house with dusty-blue siding walked a tightrope between quiet desperation and temporary stability. After the house was abandoned, a friend and I walked up the road and warily ventured inside. Half-finished coloring book pages littered the floors. Kitchen cabinets gaped open. The living room floor sagged ominously in places. Years later, nature and time have reclaimed the house, but I still sometimes wonder about the people who sheltered there. Did they find a toehold or permanently slip across the poverty line, never to return?

Runaway Fourth Grader

Sometimes you're OVER IT and need to get away! Of course, said getaway works better when no one knows where you've gone. It helps if your friend can hotwire a Jeep Laredo like she says she can. It's also better if your school bus driver doesn't drop you off at said friend's house and call your mother and tell her where you are so she can drive up the road to get you. Poor planning is why ten-year-olds fail at running away. Back home with Mom, the mood was tense, but I'd made my point. I never tried it again.

The Undertaker's Wife

When my cousin, aunt, and I visited the octogenarian who lived in an old Victorian that was once a funeral parlor, I was unnerved. At eleven, I wasn't well acquainted with death and feared that spirits might still be hanging around. While the women visited, my cousin and I explored the upstairs and touched nothing in rooms preserved in feminine charm. Elegant historical photos graced the side tables, and pastel coverlets brightened the beds. Downstairs, we avoided the parlor where bodies had been viewed, and instead enjoyed the company of the endearing old woman who was still very much alive.

Sherrie's Feathered Hair

When young women were still in the iron grip of Farrah Fawcett mania in the early eighties, I envied anyone with feathered hair. A girl named Sherrie, the epitome of casual Farrah cool, served as my counselor the one and only year I endured the abomination known as summer camp. One day, although my hair was all one length, Sherrie helped me curl it to see if we could get it to wave back on the sides. In ninety-five percent humidity, I looked cool for five minutes before the curls wilted and my hair returned to its usual mop-like style.

What's for Dinner?

When your family only shops at grocery stores, you don't think about woodland creatures as dinner fare. So when your great uncle hands your grandmother a covered roasting pot in the doorway and you sneak a peek when she cracks the lid, you're shocked to see a freshly skinned animal. Confused and revolted by its appearance, I timidly asked what it was. Squirrels don't look like squirrels without their ears and bushy tails. Without eyes and tiny paws, they look like slick hunchbacked rabbits with oversized hindquarters. We didn't stay for dinner, and I'm still curious about how it tasted.

Chin Meets Asphalt

Skateboarding is fun until you hit a pebble and the board stops but your body doesn't and you chin-plant on the asphalt. Miraculously, I didn't lose any teeth or break any bones, so I got up and wailed all the way to my front door, where my alarmed mother met me. Throughout the thirty-minute drive to the emergency room, she begged me not to fall asleep. When the doctor stuck a needle in my chin it felt like it went through my skull, and I screamed. A barely visible scar is one of the benefits of having a stay-at-home mom.

Winter Hideaway

When my great-uncle died, his white farmhouse remained unlocked. It was tucked back on a long gravel driveway up the road from my grandparents. In it, on a pool table in an unheated bedroom, my cousins and I were free to practice breaks, kiss shots, and bank shots—without adult supervision. Our breath blew frosty in the frigid room and the uneven floor caused the pool balls to roll askew, but we didn't care. Enormous sepia-toned baby portraits watched from the walls as we wiled away the hours until our fingers grew numb and we were forced to walk home.

House of Refuge

As I unrolled my sleeping bag in Kim's carpeted basement I noticed stacks of boxes, one topped with a photo
of a vibrant young blonde. Upstairs, I'd not been introduced to the despondent woman sitting at the kitchen
table; she sharply contrasted with Kim's mom, who was
confident and professional in her ivory chiffon blouse
and black skirt.

"Who was that?" I asked Kim.

"She's here because her husband beats her."

Her matter-of-fact delivery stunned me into silence.
The woman upstairs was the blonde in the picture, her life
in boxes, all of us safe in this house of refuge.

Hi Yahl

One of my cousins had nunchucks and Chinese stars back when kids could be trusted not to gouge their eyes out or maim their playmates. Looking back, it may not have been the wisest idea to buy military-grade adult weapons for a kid who was, to put it mildly, *super* energetic, but luckily no one ever got hurt. We hopped around the basement doing side kicks like Bruce Lee and flung the Chinese stars at the bare framed walls. We were ninjas who ruled the Universe until dinnertime when we had to retreat upstairs and return to life as mortals.

Faith in God and Chocolate

Some young people have terrible experiences with God. I knew Him as a benevolent guy who suffered for (sometimes) ungrateful folks. I also imagined he liked sugar, because my grandparents' church hosted an ice-cream social and cakewalk each summer. The cakes were displayed on a table and numbered wooden placards were placed in front of chairs arranged in a circle. I walked excitedly with the music and rushed to claim a chair when it stopped, but my number was never called. Despite it all, I have faith that I'll receive my German chocolate cake when I hit those pearly gates.

The Rat Warrior Queens of Benham Lane

Disclaimer: I never saw any rats, and there were never any rats in my aunt's house.

You know you're descended from tenacious women when your mother and her younger sister decide to wrap twine around their jean cuffs to keep rats from running up their legs, pick up scythes (a glorified term for machetes), and whack down a stand of tall grass and weeds that supposedly housed rats along the edge of said sister's property. When they finished, we drank iced tea and surveyed the newly shorn kingdom. Years later, I joined their Female Tenacity Club and bought a weed-eater.

Mother and Child

When the wrangler leading our trail ride stopped her horse in the ponderosa pine forest for no apparent reason, I thought something was wrong. Instead, she pointed northwest, then murmured to the person riding behind her.

In the quietest game of telephone ever, each rider turned to the next and whispered, "There's a mother and baby moose ahead. Don't make any noise as we ride by."

Luckily, the trail was a safe distance from the moose and we didn't get charged. Grateful to witness their gentle familial bond, we rode ahead, silent, as chickadees and sparrows flitted and chirped overhead.

Win, Place, Show, or Go Home Empty-Handed

Children of my generation never received participation trophies—because participation trophies didn't exist. In 4-H you won a blue, red, or white ribbon or you went home empty-handed. If you didn't win a ribbon, you didn't merit one. I was once dismissed from the arena when my horse decided to buck instead of canter. I was embarrassed and almost cried, but I learned not to quit. I rode back in to the next competition and won second place. There are no prizes for merely existing in the show ring of life; it's a painful lesson that's lost on the young.

What Would the Cops Think?

The summer my mother served as treasurer of our local Red Cross, we stuffed $30K in donated cash into paper grocery bags and wedged them behind the front seats of our red Honda that looked and drove like a roller skate. As we cruised to the bank with the windows down, I was afraid the bills would fly up in a swirling vortex of cash and we'd be pulled over by the cops. Luckily, we made it intact. I clutched my bag as we walked up the sidewalk, and the teller looked at us funny when we approached the counter.

The Cotillion Charade

I don't know how the brilliant city fathers (or more likely mothers) of Columbus, Indiana convinced the woman who ran a cotillion to stop in our town, but for a few weeks one winter, I and a room full of miserable eighth-grade victims were forced to endure painfully useless dance lessons. Quickstep. Foxtrot. Cha-cha. Waltz. I learned that fourteen-year-old boys are awkward and have bad breath. The tallest one repeatedly stepped on my toes. At school, we avoided eye contact and pretended not to know each other. The dance steps faded along with the instructor's attempts to improve my etiquette.

True Colors
1986-1992

Busing In

If we'd remained in our house in town, I could've walked to elementary, junior high, and high school. Instead we moved to the country when I was nine, and by high school I was riding three buses each way to and from school. Riding the school bus teaches you things: who's tough and who's faking it, how old you have to be to finally sit in the back with the cool kids, when to jump out of the way because a fistfight is about to erupt. Busing in taught me lessons I'd never have learned had we stayed in town.

It Was Only Dress-Up to Me

A few of my girlfriends and I used to sit in the library during study hall in high school and peruse the bridal magazines. We chose wedding gowns and invitations and made faces to rate the hideousness of bridesmaid dresses. I was drawn to the gowns and the colors, stylized calligraphy, and embossed flowers on the invitations. My friends envisioned their lives being transformed by those things, but I never did. I saw them as props in a big game of dress-up. I knew even then that my future would bring occasions that involved flowers, but never a white dress.

Gentle Heart, Iron Spine

There was one biracial couple in my high school; he was Caucasian and she was Black. I never saw any classmates antagonize them, but I'm sure they bore the brunt of judgmental stares and unforgiving comments whispered behind their backs. My hometown wasn't exactly tolerant or forward-thinking, and interracial dating wasn't widely accepted. I always believed he cherished and respected her, but when they broke up, I heard that he'd hit her. Once. I admired her for many reasons—most of all for having the gentle determination to follow her heart and the iron spine to walk away from violence.

The Patriot

Christopher was a quiet yet militant classmate who wore jean jackets with American flag patches and once teared up in speech class talking about Vietnam vets who were spat on when they returned home from the war.

If you said you didn't want to enlist, he'd snap, "You don't want to serve your country?"

He broadened his mind and discovered we were on the same side of the serve-your-country argument when I told him I could serve better by supporting those who carried guns than by actually carrying one myself.

He frowned, then finally said, "Okay. I can see that."

When Life Got Heavy

My father was once accidentally kicked in the head by his horse, who was excited to be out of the barn. Dad deflected the blow with his wrist (which inexplicably didn't break) and suffered only a crescent-shaped wound on his forehead. I grabbed my driver's permit and drove him to the hospital, where he was stitched up. He drove us home, and my maternal grandmother died the next day. I missed her funeral because my body shut down and I caught the flu (in summer) due to stress. Unlike the indelible memory of those days, Dad's scar faded and disappeared.

Basketball Makes 'Em Crazy

Indiana University won the 1987 men's NCAA basket-ball championship thanks to Keith Smart's jumper in the closing seconds. I was sixteen years old, sitting two feet away from the television and crying as if there were no tomorrow. When you're a Hoosier fan, every victory is important, and none more so than winning the Big Dance.

After the game I tried to call my aunt long distance, but instead of the phone ringing, an automated voice perfectly described the state of mind that Indiana basketball fans have when a game is on: "All circuits are busy, please try again later."

Through the Fire

In 1988, a fire destroyed nearly eight hundred thousand acres of Yellowstone National Park. My family was staying at a Montana ranch and could smell smoke as flames raged in the distance. Thankfully, early fall snows doused the fires closest to the ranch and it suffered no damage. I returned to Yellowstone several years after the inferno and was amazed by how fast the pine trees had reestablished themselves. Nature always wins; it's just a matter of how and when. I, too, can respond like nature when something tries to destroy me: give it time to heal and begin again.

Everyone Made It Out Alive

When my head jerked left and smacked the school bus window, fear seized me; I knew something horrible had happened. We'd struck the front quarter panel of Dana's truck and run over the hood. Both front truck tires were flat and gasoline was running down the road. Our bus had tilted up on two wheels, skimmed the overhead power lines, come down, and screeched to a halt. All of us dodged a bullet that day; we could've been injured, and Dana and her passenger could've died. When our bus went through that intersection the next morning, we cheered in relief.

RIP Tennessee

In high school, allegiances are shown regardless of fashion statement and gangly guys with red hair who wear bright orange satin Tennessee jackets live forever. Or at least that's what I thought when I said, "Hey, Jason," as we crossed paths in the gymnasium doorway that fateful afternoon after class. As I passed his locker the morning after the car accident, he wasn't there to shake his head out of mock disgust yet total respect for my red Indiana jacket. His locker was empty, as was a place in my heart, and my eyes watered as I walked to homeroom.

MacGyver with Masking Tape

Minutes before I was to leave for my senior prom, I started up the stairs, caught my toe, and ripped the hem and bottom of my red satin dress into a long narrow ribbon. My heart almost stopped—not going to prom was completely unfathomable. In true MacGyver fashion, my mom cut the fabric ribbon off, folded the satin under, and fashioned a new hem with masking tape. In the bathroom at the dance, my best friend gasped when I told her what had happened. Miraculously, the dress looked perfect in my prom photo, and the tape held all night.

Hidden Demons

Because Steven looked like a movie star, lots of girls wanted to date him. And because he looked like a star, played hockey, was quietly cool, and never tried too hard, we all thought his life was perfect. When he went MIA from homeroom, we never imagined his absence might be serious. I worked at the frozen yogurt shop with his girlfriend's sister, and she said he'd slit his wrists because he thought her sister was cheating on him. She wasn't. I'll never know what other hidden demons he was fighting, but his wrists healed, and he graduated on time.

Pop and Circumstance

My maternal grandfather had very specific opinions about what constituted a proper funeral. As respectful children, my mother and her siblings tried their best to honor their late father's wishes. They ordered elegant yet classy floral arrangements, a gorgeous cherry coffin, and laid his redwood cane by his side. One of my aunts asked the funeral director pre-ceremony if he had a dirty brown lightbulb because she thought the pink-tinted one in the lamp next to the casket made my grandfather look too clean. All lighting preferences aside, his funeral was spectacularly befitting of the beloved farm king he was.

Thank You for Doing Your Part

After my grandfather passed away, friends and family in his rural community brought casseroles, vegetables, and meat platters to his house after his funeral. And by meat platters, I mean enough ham to feed two counties for life.

When my parents and I communed with extended family on summer weekends, my aunt would stroll around the dinner table, place a slice of ham on everyone's plate, and say, "Thank you for doing your part."

It took over a year to empty a large chest freezer. Food is often equated with love, and people loved and missed my grandfather whole hog.

We Had a Full Tank of Gas, No Half Pack of Cigarettes, It Was Dark Outside, and We Were Not Wearing Sunglasses

Sometimes you're asked to heed a higher calling and channel the Blues Brothers. That calling came in college when one of my good friend's grandmothers passed away and I decided to drive him to and from Chicago one weekend. (I didn't tell my parents, but I was a responsible young adult—I told my aunt instead.) I saved him the bus fare home and we watched the Blackhawks win at the old Chicago Stadium. I skipped the sunglasses, but it was dark outside. Thanks to caffeinated Coca-Cola, we completed our mission from God and arrived home safely at 2:00 a.m.

Unduplicatable

One night in his dorm room on Curry 5, Lewis poured peach schnapps, a gallon of orange juice, and a bunch of other yummy-tasting alcohol into a metal trash can that had been scoured clean earlier, and everyone helped themselves with red plastic cups. That concoction was the best thing I'd ever tasted. I tried to replicate the recipe a few times (albeit in much smaller quantities), but my attempts were never quite right. Like college, some things can't, and probably shouldn't, be duplicated, no matter how hard you try, or how much orange juice and schnapps you put down.

Goodbye, My Dear Sweet Boy

In the spring of my senior year of college, my parents called to say that Stormy, the dapple-grey gelding who'd been in our family since I was four, wasn't doing well. Memories of our numerous 4-H wins and him waiting for me to get up after I'd fallen off flashed through my mind as I drove home. As he lay calmly in a thick nest of fragrant cedar shavings, I banded each end of a section of braided mane and cut it off as a keepsake. I cried all the way back to school knowing I'd lost an irreplaceable friend.

You Just Never Know About Love

Sheryl Crow was right: the first cut is the deepest. It sets the bar for what it feels like to be in love. My first love was there before real life set in with its many disappointments. He was calm and kind and always called me on my crap—nicely. He was a safe harbor, and our relationship was a place I could trust. The cut eventually healed after we amicably ended things, but a beautiful scar remained. I'm forever grateful to have been loved by him...I just didn't know it would be so long before I felt loved again.

Welcome to the Jungle
1993-2014

Drinking Game

My first job taught me that company presidents sometimes use corporate coffers as checkbooks for their pet
projects. It's impossible to respect your leaders when
they tell you that raises are minimal because they need
to cut costs, and then they turn around and donate $250K
to the University of Kentucky athletics department. To
this Indiana basketball fan, that donation felt wrong on
many levels. I worked in accounts payable when the check
request came in, and I pushed it away like a sour glass of
Kool-Aid. I never dreamed it would be a gesture I would
repeat for decades.

No Mercy

My coworker Dan had been getting sicker since November but it took doctors until spring to finally diagnose him. By then it was too late; he died in late May. Pancreatic cancer does not discriminate and is known to be hellishly devoid of mercy. It doesn't care that you're a superbly fit thirty-year-old who recently celebrated your tenth wedding anniversary and will leave behind a wife and two little boys. His loss saddened me, but I was young and didn't heed its lesson. In time, I would learn to fear a different devil that grew inside but couldn't be seen.

Strippers on a Box

On Friday nights a friend and I used to go to a bar in a mall near where we lived. Upstairs there were always two empty rectangular boxes on the raised dance floor, but no one ever danced on them (sober) until the night the strippers arrived. Two fully clad girls began dancing suggestively close to each other, which drew attention and men to them like flies to honey. The girls learned they had sixty to ninety seconds to toss out business cards before being escorted out of the bar. I admired their boldness and the power of in-person networking.

Under the Knife

In 2000, my voice started sounding raspy and would often cut out. I thought I had a cold and ignored my worsening condition. My dad was concerned, and because father knows best, I saw a throat specialist. What ensued was a decade-long battle with the recurring growths on my vocal cords that resulted in fifteen surgeries, sometimes two a year. Who doesn't take speaking for granted? Who doesn't take *breathing* for granted? Vocal cord growths slowly block off your airway. Twice when I tried to speak after surgery, I could only croak. Without modern medicine I would've died at twenty-nine.

Was That a 12-Gauge?

We buried my mamaw on a cold, damp morning as the wind tried to clear the clouds from the mottled sky. She'd been slowly losing the battle against dementia for months and ended up sick at the nursing home before passing away at the hospital a few days later. While the minister spoke I looked around the cemetery that holds several of my other relatives for safekeeping. As I watched a flock of blackbirds lift skyward, I heard shots in the distance.

All I could think was "Someone is going to have squirrel for lunch."

And "I am definitely home."

Jackson

Your boss is having a tough day when he has to lay you off even though he doesn't want to. He's having a tough year when he calls weeks later to say the guy who sat across the aisle from you committed suicide.

I'll never know what made Jackson end his life. He'd stopped drinking and reconnected with an old girlfriend, and they were thinking about getting back together.

The bright fuchsia Christmas cactus he'd gifted me five months earlier lived for another fifteen years. When it died I felt as if I'd lost him again, this time for good.

Great White Bear

When I told my father I wanted to visit polar bears in Canada, he laughed. He didn't laugh six years later when Mom and I boarded a plane to Canada. She and I traveled to Churchill, Manitoba, where we saw several bears and visited the hockey rink/hospital/school building. We watched the ghostly green northern lights through our hotel room window, sitting on my bed in our nightgowns. I came nose to nose with a bear through a tundra buggy window. When a species may go extinct, you use that urgency to board the plane and quit worrying about others' opinions.

Praying to the Porcelain God

When my first Ménière's attack hit I knelt on the cold tile bathroom floor at work, vomited until I could only gasp, and wondered what man in the office would be strong enough to carry me to my car. Months later—after my third attack—my boss buried his head in the sand, ignored my incompetent coworker, and saddled me with her job. I torched my misplaced loyalty, called bullshit, and resigned. Taking one hundred percent responsibility for your life and career can be excruciating. Quitting was one of the best decisions I've ever made and one I've never regretted.

Lost and Found

Undeterred by drizzle, I stood in Moose Creek at the back of Denali National Park. As I filtered water through a rubberized pan, I wondered how miners a century ago felt as their lives dripped away in search of the mother lode. I wrapped the gold flake I found in paper, but the gold was gone when I unfolded the paper at the lodge. I lamented its loss and the girl behind the counter found it and extricated it from my coat pocket seam with her fingernails. A miner's life is filled with the discoveries of heartbreak, exhilaration, and relief.

The Big Five

Moose, caribou, grizzly bears, Dall sheep, and wolves are Denali's five must-see animals. During my three-day visit, I tried to keep my expectations low. I wanted to see grizzly bears; seeing the other four animals would be a bonus. On the slow, picturesque seven-hour ride over the sixty miles to Kantishna, we saw moose, caribou, sheep, and several grizzlies. On the ride out two days later our bus rounded a corner and we were stunned to see a wolf trotting along the gravel road. He was so close that if we'd opened the bus door, he might have climbed on.

Turning Forty

I took myself to a bistro and wine bar for takeout the night I turned forty. I ordered a Caesar salad, the scallop entrée, and chocolate cake. Coincidentally, the entire meal cost $40, including tip. Back home, I enjoyed my dinner and watched the Avalanche beat the Lightning on TV. My mother called to wish me a happy birthday, I opened my presents, and I was in bed by 9:15. It wasn't until three months later that I awoke with my heart pounding and realized that I might have tipped over the summit of midlife at thirty-eight and missed it.

The Outdoorsman

I should've known I'd never be happy with one career. My papaw died when I was eight and from the stories I've heard, I wish I could've known him better. He grew tobacco. He hunted raccoons with hounds by moonlight and flashlight and sold their pelts to fur traders on the Ohio River. He was the foreman of a road crew that built a state highway. The one thing he couldn't do was work inside; being cooped up didn't suit his outdoor nature. He made a life out of doing what he loved and inspired me to do the same.

What Do You Want in Your Box?

When my uncle passed away, he left behind a detailed list of items that my mother and her sisters dutifully placed around the inside edges of his casket. (Personalized interior decoration is an apparently overlooked revenue stream for funeral homes.) Shortly after I turned forty, I woke up in a sweat thanks to a nightmare about me rotting in a box. I interpreted this to mean that I can't be cold too long before they cremate me. It's also probably why I haven't given my list much thought. My instructions will read: Incinerate, ship, and scatter outside Yellowstone National Park.

Past Lives

Many people don't believe in past lives. Given everything that's happened to me, I may still be living a few of them in this lifetime. When you feel connected on a soul level to a place, you can't always explain why. There's no rational reason why I feel at home every time I visit Yellowstone National Park, but the vision of me as a solitary trapper/ mountain man tromping around in the late 1800s comes to mind. Other than that inconvenient volcano situation, Yellowstone has it all: fresh water, big game, sunshine, and shelter. Who knows? Maybe I'm Jim Bridger reincarnated.

Wolf at My Suburban Door

My mother told me I'd regret removing the metal mesh that covered the split-rail fence along the back of my property. I tore it out to prevent tumbleweed orgies and so I could quickly weed eat the fence line without getting the weed eater string tangled up in the mesh. When a lone coyote trotted past my sliding glass door one rainy morning, my heart skipped a beat, and I remembered her admonishment. When we tear down our barriers, scary uninvited creatures sometimes get in. But if those barriers remained in place, we'd never feel the thrill of surviving them.

I'm (Not Really) Sorry for
Not Paying Attention

Good corporate meetings led to decisions that solved problems. Bad meetings turned into Kumbaya Love Ins, which were the enemy of productivity and often resulted in me losing an hour of my life never to get it back. To rebel against this injustice, I quit paying attention during bad meetings and used that time to invent creative solutions to plot and character issues that plagued one of my in-progress novels.

I once left a finance meeting giddy and whispered to a coworker and fellow writer, "I know how she's going to die."

She laughed. It was an hour well spent.

Slip Slidin' Away
2015-Present

Awash in the Sea

When I won the lucky ticket out of corporate America, I quickly realized I didn't miss it, and it wouldn't miss me. Numbers would be crunched. Useless data would be pushed. People would still fret unnecessarily over inconsequential decisions that wouldn't be recalled in a week, let alone a month. I was excited to finally be let go but bitter about how much of my life had been lost to irrelevance. The double-edged sword of being laid off is that it simultaneously liberates you but then makes you question your worth. Eventually, not being needed became a gift named freedom.

Devastating Discovery

"Were you here earlier when the policeman was here?" my father asked matter-of-factly after I'd ignored all speed limits and driven—gripped in fear—from my house to his that afternoon.

I assured him kindly; I hadn't. Unfazed by a policeman bringing him home and not remembering I hadn't been there were the tip of the iceberg. Shriveled food sat in the fridge. Paper plates rested in the sink. He'd had food poisoning for nine days. I fed him soup, and my mom flew back home to Colorado from Indiana the next day. We moved him out twenty months later.

The Crying Months

August and September were The Crying Months. In my car, in bed at night, or as I meandered down grocery aisles, tears would well in my eyes as I thought about the unknown months ahead. Nothing had been confirmed, but I knew what was coming; my father's mind was faltering, and his journey would be a one-way ticket down a terrifying and difficult road. His eventual Parkinson's diagnosis was a shock; the accompanying dementia diagnosis was not. The Crying Months were a slog through a dark tunnel filled with fear and sorrow. When they faded, what remained was uneasy acceptance.

Long Slow Decline

No one knows why my father's brain decided to slowly devour itself. He had no head injuries, no stroke, and no related medical conditions. The hard truth was that my mother and I weren't surprised; his mother's mind had betrayed her, too. Dad took a retirement package at fifty. He earned a BFA in Painting, a lifelong dream. He fly fished and painted, but those became too much, and he gave them up. Not having anything to do and not having to do anything are a double dose of the same poisonous pill. Taken long enough, the prescription is fatal.

Resurrection Day

After three years, my gut told me things weren't going to work, and I needed to end it with S. I no longer wanted a long-distance relationship. We were too far apart, in different places, literally and figuratively. He was understanding. Time weighs the gravity of all decisions. In the moment, I had no regrets, but as years passed and I found myself not connecting with anyone, I started to question whether I'd thrown away my chance at love. Would I feel that spark again? Relief flooded me when R and I talked at Starbucks, and the answer became YES.

False Start

Because relationship false starts stink, it's sometimes hard to force yourself to learn from them. I was correct in believing R was a good man, but made the mistake of ignoring my instinct that said he was afraid to be in a relationship. Despite hating texting, I discovered I need semi-regular communication to feel connected and secure. My expectations around where a fifty-two-year-old "should" live (hint: *not* in a rented room in a house with two others) left me mired in unshakable judgment.

False starts show you what you need to know, even if you struggle to accept their lessons.

Om Shanti Harmonium Style

My hatha yoga class became instantly intriguing when I walked into the studio and spotted a Linus-size piano with an accordion attached to its back sitting on the floor. As we lay in Shavasana at the end of class, our instructor, Wolf (an energetic blonde pixie sprite with cropped hair and a melodic voice), explained that she liked to sing to close the hour. She played her harmonium and sang the song's first stanza, then invited us to sit up and join her. In near darkness, we finished the song; I've never left a yoga class so full of joy.

The Hardest Thing

Being a boss lady writer is the hardest thing I've ever willingly chosen to do. I thought I understood how tough it'd be—turns out I was delusional. Entrepreneurship forces one hundred percent responsibility on you in ways you never expect and doesn't give a crap whether you succeed or fail. It forces you so far out of your comfort zone that you swear that zone is on another continent and will require a passport for reentry. Being a business owner continuously builds you up and tears you down, but it's a choice that rewards me, even on tough days.

My Sign is Binders

When I left my first corporate job to move to Colorado, I took stock of what I'd left behind. It amounted to four years of financial reports—which wouldn't be looked at again—filed in binders. I concluded the same thing when I was blessedly released from my last corporate job, thus ending my illustrious twenty-two-year career. As I hole-punched pages of an in-progress manuscript, the delicious irony hit me. I'm a writer, and if I died tomorrow, guess what people would have to clean out of my house? Whether filled with words or numbers, binders are my astrological sign.

But is It Occult?

In 2015, I joined a tarot card Meetup group. I'd been drawn to the artistry and colors of the cards but had no idea how they worked; I was curious and hoped the group could help me. So when my mom asked if tarot was occult, I didn't know what to say. Technically, I think it is, but tarot for me is about awareness, not divination. I don't lead séances in my living room, invoke spells, or chant naked on my coffee table. Instead, I use the cards to look inward and illuminate the answers I know are already there.

House of Doors

"It's hard to live in a house that's not really a house, you know?" my father lamented as we sat on the living room couch one afternoon.

I paused to consider how to reply to such a nonsensical statement.

"That must be frustrating," I said.

"It really is," he replied, then let the subject drop.

He'd complained about the many doors in the house, and he wasn't wrong. There are sixteen—all wooden sliders, singles, and doubles. It crushed me to think of how dispirited he must've felt each time he opened one only to find things but not memories.

Without You, I Would Be Nothing

One afternoon as my father battled Parkinson's and dementia, my mother helped him inside, where they stood in the hall and admired his vivid rose garden through the window.

After a few moments, he turned to her and said, "Without you, I would be nothing."

Not only was it the literal observation of a man who could no longer care for himself, but I wonder if it was also his final admission of gratefulness: for their fifty-plus years of marriage, for the role she played in our lives, for the ties that would soon be unbound by his impending demise.

Wondering

When my mother checked my father into the locked memory care unit, he asked, "Where are you going to take me next, an institution?"

Apparently his single room with faux hardwood laminate floors and a handicapped-equipped bathroom didn't strike him as "institutional." He never understood why he couldn't go home, but he never asked, "Where are you going to take me next?" again.

He napped more as time passed, and his Sundowner's behavior increased. I visited him once a month, always wondering if he ever finally accepted where he was and whether he wanted to go on living or not.

I'm Just Delighted to See You

The first time I visited my father in the memory care unit, I found him dozing in a chair. I sat down next to him and gently tapped his arm.

He looked at me with recognition and surprise, then asked, "How did you get here?"

"Mom brought me," I said.

His next words greeted me each time I returned to visit for the next five months: "Well, I'm just delighted to see you."

Driving home, I always felt like I was running away from fear and what was to come. But each time Dad remembered me, I, too, was delighted.

Below the Horizon Line

If this astrology business is to be believed, I'm completely screwed. I was born at night (on my due date and after work hours, but before bedtime so as to not inconvenience anyone), and my sun lies below the horizon line along with seven of ten remaining planets. According to a reference book, my keyword is "inner aim," which means "primary motivation for achievement is to satisfy themselves." Venus, Mars, and Jupiter dance in Scorpio with Neptune and Mercury next door in Sagittarius. I'm the lone wolf introvert; my life is an opportunity to spread laughter and intrigue through writing.

Year of the Pig

On a lark, I dug out all nineteen of my journals and reread them over one long weekend. For some, this exercise might sound like slow torture, but I was on a quest. Covers of robin's-egg blue suede, and etched mahogany and floral embossed leather all housed pages separated by red satin ribbons. On them were scribbled the repeated pleadings of my soul: write more, consider therapy, find work you love. And so I have. I write regularly, attend therapy, and my author journey continues. I wander the tall grass, much like a pig on safari, rooting for tasty morsels.

Oblivion

My father lost consciousness on a Wednesday, and my mother and I visited him in the memory care unit the next day. She swabbed his lips with water as we said hello. On Saturday we returned, and his breath rattled with the sound of death. Beneath the sheet, he'd been reduced to a thin being in a white shirt whose chest would sometimes fail to rise, then spring to life again, causing my heart to seize with terror each time his breathing paused. At home, we organized his clothes for cremation from the socks up, uncertain he'd survive the weekend.

The Day He Died

I wasn't at the care unit the morning my father died. In retrospect, I can't say why I didn't accompany my mother to visit him that sunny Monday other than the mundaneness of life, the thought of the hour drive home, all my way of avoiding what was coming. My mother called that afternoon. She'd arrived to find him gasping, and not ten minutes after she'd introduced herself and held his hand, he'd passed. She'd coordinated his removal from the care unit, gone to her sewing group, not told them, and returned home. We all kept our commitments that day.

Eclipse My Heart

My mother scheduled my father's private viewing two days before a solar eclipse would darken parts of Wyoming and drop the temperature in Denver ten degrees at midday. We placed patches from his Army days on his shoulders and laid a burgundy rose on his chest. His slightly sunken face made him look eerily like his late mother.

My mother picked up his hand twice, and I wanted to shout, "Leave the man in peace!"

The morning of the eclipse, I drove back to Denver, caught in northbound traffic, trying to outrun my own darkness and that of the sun.

Legacies

Indiana welcomed me home with ninety-degree temperatures and a sticky heat index of one hundred five during the September my mother and I returned for my father's interment. Immediate family sat on folding chairs covered with sapphire-blue velour beneath the white tent at his service. Behind us, friends and relatives gathered as the late morning sun beat down. Afterward, second cousins left to bale hay, and everyone else lunched at a historic farm near the state highway my father's father helped build in the early twentieth century. Across the miles, Indiana is still my beacon of tradition and living legacies.

Discernment

Months after my father's funeral, my mother and I boxed up what remained of his art studio. I discovered his pencil sketches from high school, both of his Indiana diplomas (but not the one from Harvard), and an application he sent to the Famous Artists School in 1969. What he'd written on several saved note cube squares was heart-wrenching; I learned more about him from those notes than I did in all our conversations. I've tried to stay connected to him by tucking seventy-seven years of mementos into the monogrammed *Mad Men*–era briefcase he carried to work each day.

Travelers

"At some point, you become your ancestors." These were my father's words as he and my mother sat by my bedside in my parents' guest room during the summer I was first diagnosed with Ménière's.

Severe vertigo had pinned me to the bed, and it'd be another few hours before I could hold down food. With Ménière's under control, I walk the road of life, a few paces ahead of Parkinson's, dementia, and heart disease. I refuse to let them stalk me; instead, I respect them as possible travel partners and insist they always stay at least one step behind.

Inanimate Objects of Desire

The woman who wrote the book on Swedish death cleaning is onto something. When my mother passes away, I'll be left with a combined three cars, two houses, seven beds, and five sets of china. Forced to answer the competing questions of what is trivial and what is most valuable, my mother purges her house slowly and with much thought. Each month, she sets a bag or two of items out on the curb for the donation truck to pick up. When she's gone, I'll take over the great purge surrounded by an ocean of objects that have outlived her.

The Zeros and the Fives

Many people fear the zero birthdays. I don't put much faith in arbitrary numbers, but interesting life patterns have emerged over the years. At twenty-five, I struggled with depression and boredom. At thirty, I finished my MBA and loved living in Colorado. At thirty-five, I had survived ten throat surgeries and was unemployed. Forty excited me, and I enjoyed my job. By forty-five, I was burning through savings and trying to build a business. I recently turned half a hundred and have published two books. It's tricky, but I'm trying to stay positive as I head toward the next five.

How Long Remains

Forget turning the big five-o. My most urgent concern is how long do I have left? I gave this serious thought in my mid forties and the answer did not ease my anxiety. Do I have thirty-four, thirty-seven, or forty years—which feels too long? More importantly, what do I want to experience as my expiration date draws closer? For some reason, three or four decades only feels like enough time to walk to the bathroom and back twice. When you're young, you're going to live forever. When your youth fades, the clock ticks ever louder as time winds down.

The Ultimate Choice

As I read *The Orphan Adult*, I realized that life really does move at warp speed. It zips along just as it did when I was two, up on that horse with the lady wrangler in Montana. When my mother dies, I may still have cousins and a few aunts and uncles left, but technically I'll be an orphan.

After I finished the book, I decided that no one is an orphan unless they choose to be. I'll create a new family, tied by blood and choice, and live out my days surrounded by the people and places I love.

Acknowledgments

Firstly, I'm grateful for my brain, which was inexplicably able to dial up all of these sometimes funny, sometimes heart-wrenching moments over my half century of life.

On a more serious note, thanks go to Sun Cooper and Aric Queen for giving the initial manuscript of this book a first pass and encouraging me to revise and publish it. Their support and superb feedback helped me shape each micro-memoir and the book as a whole into something powerful and authentic. Meghan Pinson and Rhonda Erb were instrumental in providing expert copyediting and publishing advice.

Additional thanks go to my mother and my Aunt Louise for reviewing an early draft and providing highly biased yet valuable feedback.

Brandi McCann masterfully used a photo of my gleeful tiny human self that was taken shortly before my first birthday to create a cover that captures my irrepressible spirit.

Thank you most of all, dear readers, for making this work worthwhile. I so hope you enjoyed these recollections of my life and that they made you reflect on the indelible memories that have shaped yours. Thanks as well to librarians and booksellers who connect readers to new stories and personal histories each day. Without you, our world would be a much duller place.

Lastly, I'm grateful for my parents, who gave me the opportunity to have so many of these adventures. I hold no greater truth than the title of this book: Without you, I would be nothing.

About the Author

Brooke L. Davis is a writer and wellness coach in Colorado. When she isn't plotting shenanigans for her next novel, she can be found watching sports, hiking and taking photographs in the mountains of Colorado and Montana, and reading tarot. A native of Indiana, she has called Colorado home for over twenty years.

Visit Brooke on the web at:
www.brookedaviswrites.com
Instagram: @brooke.davis.writes

www.ingramcontent.com/pod-product-compliance
Lightning Source LLC
Chambersburg PA
CBHW070811050426
42452CB00011B/1991